For Philip – M. J.
For Edward – R. J.

This is a book about a pair of squirrels, and it is also a book about the seasons and how the weather changes through the year. As you read this book with a child, you may want to discuss the following concepts:

There are seasons because the earth is tilted in its orbit around the sun. When the northern half of the earth is tilted away from the sun, it is winter there. The days are shorter and the sun stays low in the sky, and its rays have to travel farther through the atmosphere to reach the ground. This makes it cold. At the same time, the southern half of the earth is tilted toward the sun, so it is summer there. The days are longer and more heat from the sun reaches the ground. This makes it hotter. When the northern half of the earth is tilted toward the sun, the opposite is true.

Clouds are made of tiny drops of water. If those drops join together into larger, heavier drops, they fall to the ground as rain. When the air is colder, the drops may form snowflakes instead.

Both moisture and warmth are needed for thunderstorms, which is why thunderstorms happen most often in the summer. Thunder is the noise made by lightning.

The Squirrels' Busy Year

Martin Jenkins

illustrated by
Richard Jones

It's winter.

It's cold! The sun is low in the sky, the pond is
frozen, and there's snow on the ground.
It's very quiet. In a hole in the trunk of a big tree
perches an owl, keeping an eye on things.

Not too far away, two squirrels are curled
up in their cozy nest. They can't stay there
forever, though. They'll soon get hungry,
and then they'll need to go out
to find something to eat.

They'd better get a move on. It will soon be dark.

Down the trunk . . .
over to the stump . . .
a quick dig, and yes!
Some acorns.

It's snowing again.
Time to get back to the nest.

It's spring.

It's warm. The ice and snow have all gone. It's noisy! There are birds singing in the bushes, and the pond is full of frogs croaking loudly. Not all the birds are making noise, though. In the hole in the big tree the owl is sitting quietly, still keeping an eye on things.

The squirrels are out and about, looking for food.

The acorns are all gone, but there are
fat, juicy buds on the maple trees.

The sun is setting,
but the squirrels are
still busy.

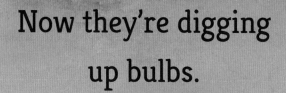

Now they're digging
up bulbs.

Whoosh!

That was close!
The owl almost got them!

It's summer.

It's hot. The frogs are keeping cool in the pond.
It's quiet and still. The squirrels are lazing about,
staying out of the sun. And up in the big tree,
in his hole in the trunk, sits
the owl.

The clouds are getting bigger.
The sky is darkening, and
there's a wind blowing.
Rumble rumble.
What was that?
Thunder!

Rumble rumble. Crack!

Lightning has struck the big tree!

Did the owl get away? Yes!

It's fall.

It's a bit chilly. The frogs have disappeared, but they
haven't gone far: they're sleeping in the
mud at the bottom of the pond.

Most of the birds have flown off to spend the winter somewhere warmer. The owl is still around, though.

The squirrels are busy
picking up acorns.

Every now and then
they eat one or two . . .

but mostly they just
carry them off, one after
another after another, and
bury them in the ground.

In a few weeks it will be winter again, and there might be snow. Most of the time the squirrels will be tucked up in their nest . . .
but occasionally they'll have to go out to find something to eat.

THINKING ABOUT
SEASONS AND WEATHER

We divide the year into four seasons: winter, spring, summer, and fall. Which season is the coldest? Which season is the hottest? What season is it where you live right now?

Can you find examples of different types of weather in the book? Look for rain, snow, and thunder and lightning. All of these types of weather come from clouds!

Animals survive the winter cold in different ways: some find a cozy place to sleep, others travel to warmer parts of the world, and some just tough it out! What do each of the different animals in this story do during the winter?

What happens to the water in a pond when it's really cold? Put a small amount of water in a cup and put it in your freezer overnight. What has the water turned into?

INDEX

Look up the pages to find out about seasons and weather.

Text copyright © 2018 by Martin Jenkins
Illustrations copyright © 2018 by Richard Jones

First U.S. edition 2018

Library of Congress Catalog Card Number pending
ISBN 978-0-7636-9600-9

24 25 26 27 CCP 10 9 8 7 6 5 4

Printed in Shenzhen, Guangdong, China

This book was typeset in Kreon.
The illustrations were done in mixed media.

Candlewick Press
99 Dover Street
Somerville, Massachusetts 02144

visit us at www.candlewick.com

CANDLEWICK PRESS